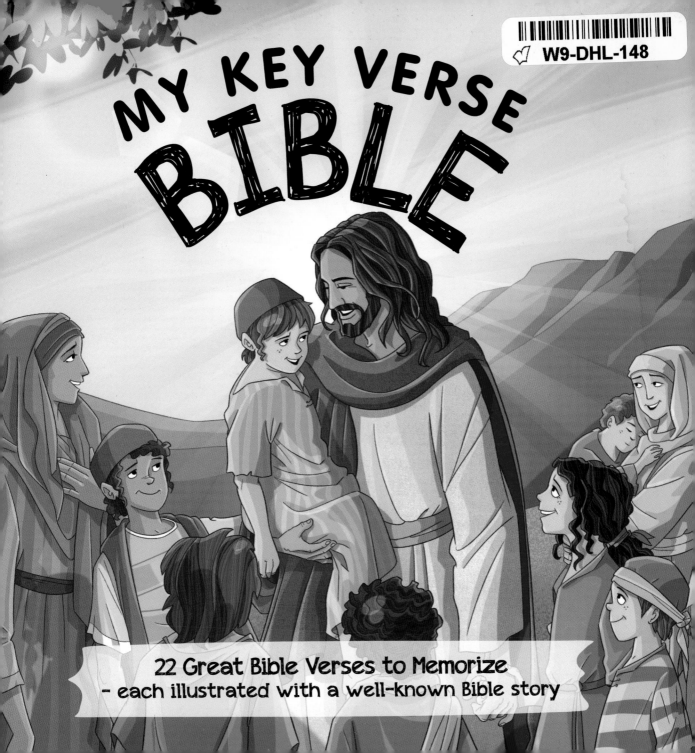

# MY KEY VERSE BIBLE

22 Great Bible Verses to Memorize
- each illustrated with a well-known Bible story

# CONTENTS

**Perfectly Created**
I praise you because I am fearfully and wonderfully made. ...................................................6

**Nothing to Fear**
Do not be afraid, for I am with you. .................................................................10

**A God Who Cares**
Give all your worries and cares to God, for He cares about you. (NLT) ...................14

**God's Good Plan**
"For I know the plans I have for you," declares the Lord, "plans to prosper you and not to harm you, plans to give you hope and a future." ..................................18

**God's Ways Are Best**
Trust in the Lord with all your heart and lean not on your own understanding. ...............22

**A Brave General**
Be strong and courageous. Do not be terrified; do not be discouraged, for the Lord your God will be with you wherever you go. .....................................26

**Daring to Ask**
Ask and it will be given to you; seek and you will find; knock and the door will be opened to you. ...................30

**The Shepherd Boy and Warrior King**
The Lord is my shepherd, I have all that I need. (NLT) .....................................34

**A Beautiful Queen Saves a Nation**
Don't worry about anything, instead pray about everything. (NLT) ......................38

**Fearless Love**
Love the Lord your God with all your heart and with all your soul and with all your strength. ..........................42

**God's Forgiveness**
The Lord is good to all; He has compassion on all He has made. ...........................46

## A Savior Is Born
Come, let us bow down in worship, let us kneel before the Lord our Maker. ...............................50

## Give Thanks
Give thanks to the Lord, for He is good; His love endures forever. .....................................54

## Costly Kindness
Do to others as you would have them do to you. ..........................................................58

## Forgive Each Other
Be kind and compassionate to one another, forgiving each other, just as in Christ God forgave you. ...............62

## Come to Me
"Let the little children come to me, and do not hinder them, for the Kingdom of God belongs to such as these" .....66

## Forgiven and Free
He has removed our sins as far from us as the east is from the west. .....................................70

## Jesus Made a Way
For God so loved the world that He gave His one and only Son, that whoever believes in Him shall not perish but have eternal life. ................................................................................74

## Jesus Is Alive!
"I am the resurrection and the life. Anyone who believes in me will live, even after dying." (NLT) .............78

## God Takes Care of His Followers
But seek first His kingdom and His righteousness, and all these things will be given to you as well. ...........82

## Changed by the Truth
If we believe that Jesus is truly Christ, we are God's children (CEV). ...................................86

## Sing Praise to God
Rejoice in the Lord always. I will say it again: Rejoice! ...............................................90

I praise you because
I am fearfully and
wonderfully made.

Psalm 139:14

## Perfectly Created

After God created the universe—earth and sky, sun, moon, stars, and all living creatures—He made man. He gathered some soil and shaped the first human to look like Himself. God created the man in his image. Then God blew His breath of life into Adam and he came alive. Adam was wonderfully made by a perfect God. God was pleased with all He had created and saw that it was good.

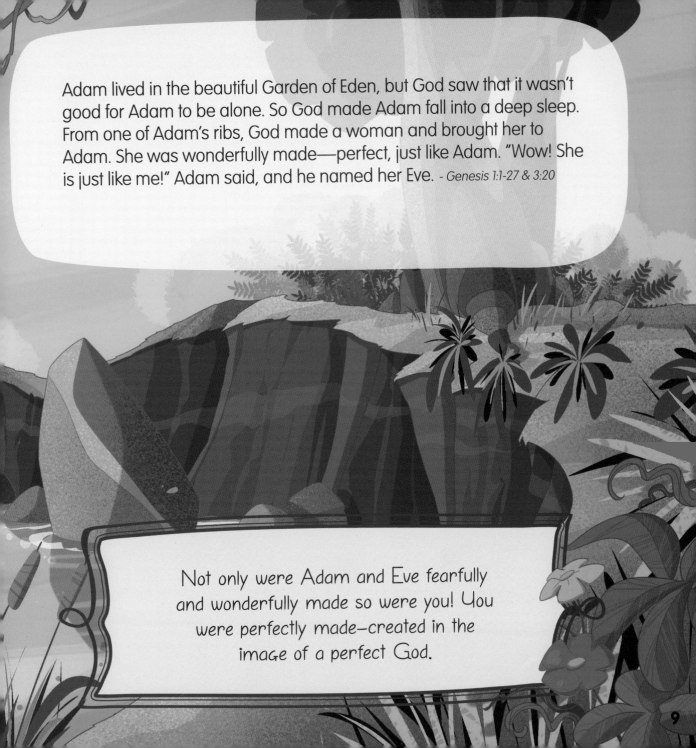

Adam lived in the beautiful Garden of Eden, but God saw that it wasn't good for Adam to be alone. So God made Adam fall into a deep sleep. From one of Adam's ribs, God made a woman and brought her to Adam. She was wonderfully made—perfect, just like Adam. "Wow! She is just like me!" Adam said, and he named her Eve. *- Genesis 1:1-27 & 3:20*

Not only were Adam and Eve fearfully and wonderfully made so were you! You were perfectly made—created in the image of a perfect God.

Do not be afraid,
for I am with you.

Isaiah 43:5

10

## Nothing to Fear

In the beautiful world God made, everyone had become wicked. This made God sad, and He decided to put an end to it all. But one man still loved God, so God said to him: "Noah, build an ark big enough for your family and two of each animal. I am going to send a flood to destroy everything on earth. Don't be afraid. I will keep you and your family safe." Noah did as God said, and even when the thunder and rainstorms came, Noah, his family, and the animals were safe in the ark.

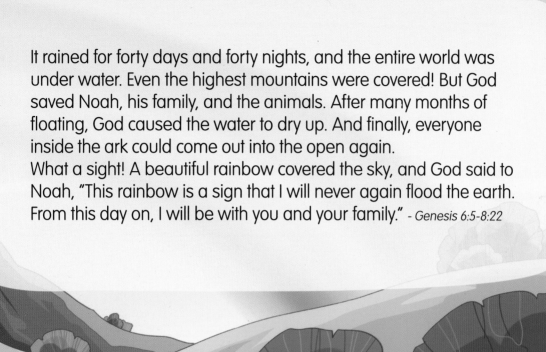

It rained for forty days and forty nights, and the entire world was under water. Even the highest mountains were covered! But God saved Noah, his family, and the animals. After many months of floating, God caused the water to dry up. And finally, everyone inside the ark could come out into the open again.
What a sight! A beautiful rainbow covered the sky, and God said to Noah, "This rainbow is a sign that I will never again flood the earth. From this day on, I will be with you and your family." *- Genesis 6:5-8:22*

Even when the flood destroyed everything on Earth and the rain still came pouring, God stood by His promise to Noah and kept him safe. God will keep this promise to you and keep you safe, too.

Give all your worries and cares to God, for He cares about you.

1 Peter 5:7 (NLT)

## A God Who Cares

Abraham was a friend of God, and God had blessed him with everything he could ask for—except a child. "Who will inherit my possessions?" Abraham wondered. Without a child, Abraham would be a faint memory after he died, and his family line would end. This was heavy on Abraham's heart, but God had a plan. One night God said to Abraham, "Look at the stars and count them." This was impossible for Abraham because the sky was filled with innumerable twinkling lights. "This is how it will be with your family," God said. "They will be as many as the stars."

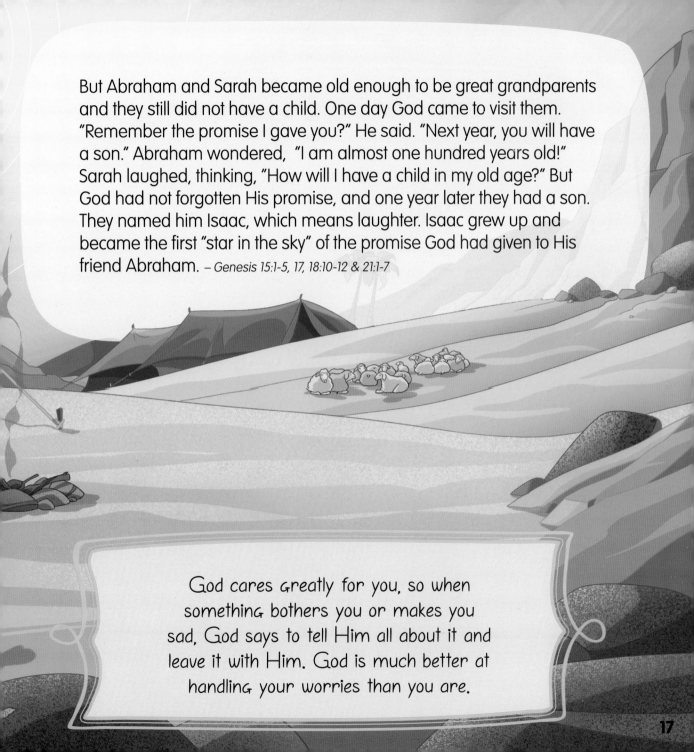

But Abraham and Sarah became old enough to be great grandparents and they still did not have a child. One day God came to visit them. "Remember the promise I gave you?" He said. "Next year, you will have a son." Abraham wondered, "I am almost one hundred years old!" Sarah laughed, thinking, "How will I have a child in my old age?" But God had not forgotten His promise, and one year later they had a son. They named him Isaac, which means laughter. Isaac grew up and became the first "star in the sky" of the promise God had given to His friend Abraham. *– Genesis 15:1-5, 17, 18:10-12 & 21:1-7*

God cares Greatly for you, so when something bothers you or makes you sad, God says to tell Him all about it and leave it with Him. God is much better at handling your worries than you are.

"For I know the plans I have for you," declares the LORD, "plans to prosper you and not to harm you, plans to give you hope and a future."

Jeremiah 29:11

## God's Good Plan

Joseph's father, Jacob, loved Joseph very much. In fact, Jacob loved Joseph more than his older brothers and one day he gave him a beautiful coat made of rich colored cloth. This special attention made Joseph's older brothers jealous, and they hated him. One day, Joseph told his brothers, "I dreamed that all of you would bow down to me one day and that I would be the greatest one of all." Joseph's brothers hated him even more. "Who does he think he is?" they thought. One day they decided to get rid of him, so they trapped him in a pit and sold him as a slave!

Joseph ended up working as a slave in Egypt and was even thrown into prison unjustly. Many years later God let Joseph help the Pharaoh, and he was put in charge of saving Egypt from a great famine. With God's wisdom, Joseph managed to do just that. People from different countries came to Joseph to buy food. One day Joseph met some foreigners who bowed down to him and asked if they could buy food. Joseph realized these men were his brothers. Joseph was overjoyed to see them and said "You wanted to send me away because you hated me, but God actually sent me here to save our lives!" - *Genesis 37, 42:1-8 & 45:1-15*

When you are disappointed and sad when things turn out differently than you wanted them to, trust that God is mighty enough to turn it into something good in time.

Trust in the Lord with all your heart and lean not on your own understanding.

Proverbs 3:5

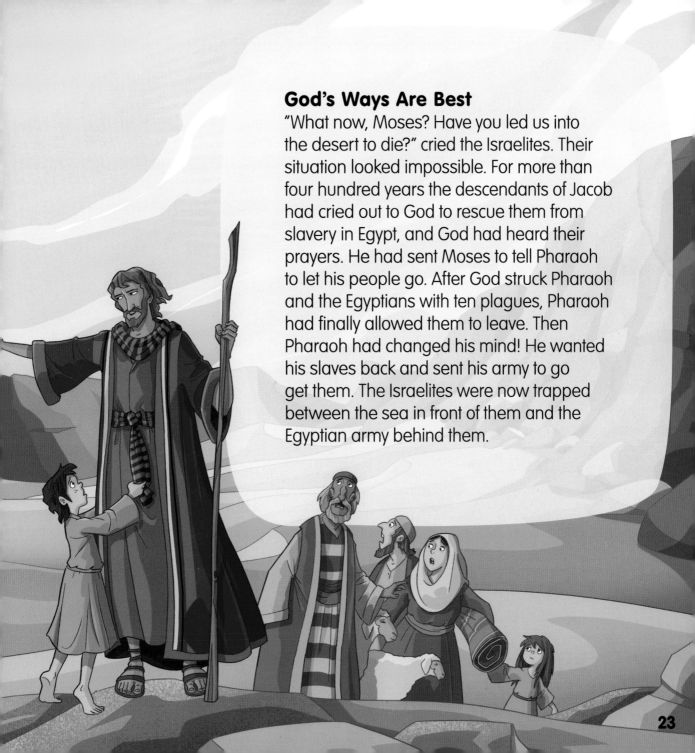

## God's Ways Are Best

"What now, Moses? Have you led us into the desert to die?" cried the Israelites. Their situation looked impossible. For more than four hundred years the descendants of Jacob had cried out to God to rescue them from slavery in Egypt, and God had heard their prayers. He had sent Moses to tell Pharaoh to let his people go. After God struck Pharaoh and the Egyptians with ten plagues, Pharaoh had finally allowed them to leave. Then Pharaoh had changed his mind! He wanted his slaves back and sent his army to go get them. The Israelites were now trapped between the sea in front of them and the Egyptian army behind them.

But Moses said, "Today God will rescue us!" He stretched out his staff over the Red Sea, as God had told him. Then God drove back the sea and dried up the ground. The Israelites walked through the sea on dry ground, a wall of water on the right and on the left. After the Israelites reached the other shore, the water crashed down on the Egyptian army. God had come to the rescue, and saved the Israelites from a life in slavery in Egypt! - *Exodus 14:5-28*

At times God might answer your prayer in a way that seems like the Red Sea is parting for you! Other times it is much less miraculous. But because God loves you, you can trust that His ways are always best.

Be strong and courageous. Do not be terrified; do not be discouraged, for the Lord your God will be with you wherever you go.

Joshua 1:9

26

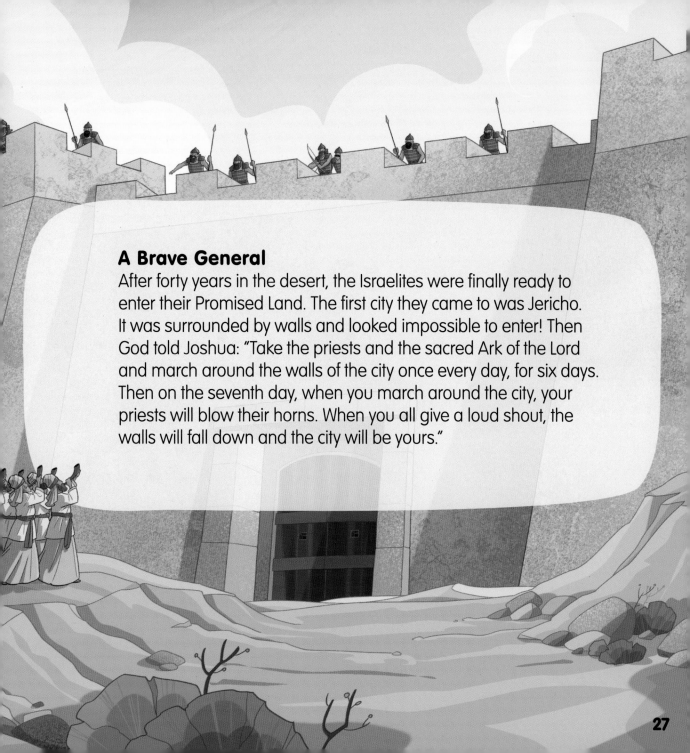

## A Brave General

After forty years in the desert, the Israelites were finally ready to enter their Promised Land. The first city they came to was Jericho. It was surrounded by walls and looked impossible to enter! Then God told Joshua: "Take the priests and the sacred Ark of the Lord and march around the walls of the city once every day, for six days. Then on the seventh day, when you march around the city, your priests will blow their horns. When you all give a loud shout, the walls will fall down and the city will be yours."

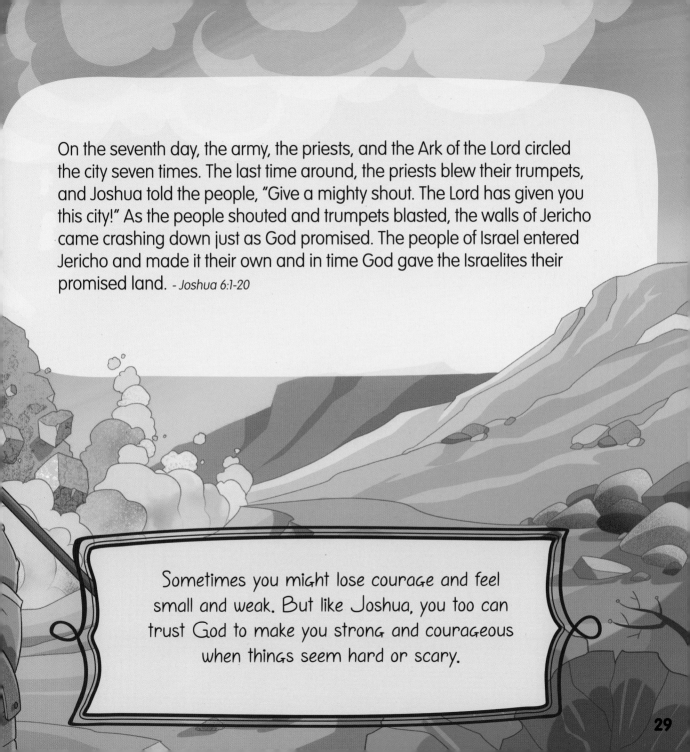

On the seventh day, the army, the priests, and the Ark of the Lord circled the city seven times. The last time around, the priests blew their trumpets, and Joshua told the people, "Give a mighty shout. The Lord has given you this city!" As the people shouted and trumpets blasted, the walls of Jericho came crashing down just as God promised. The people of Israel entered Jericho and made it their own and in time God gave the Israelites their promised land. - *Joshua 6:1-20*

Sometimes you might lose courage and feel small and weak. But like Joshua, you too can trust God to make you strong and courageous when things seem hard or scary.

Ask and it will be given to you;
seek and you will find; knock and
the door will be opened to you.

Matthew 7:7

## Daring to Ask

Ruth and Naomi had lost their family. Now they had returned home to Israel after living many years in the country of Moab. But they were poor and had no one to take care of them, so Ruth told Naomi, "Let me find a field that is being harvested, and I will pick up the leftover grain behind the harvesters." The field Ruth began gathering grain in belonged to a man named Boaz. Boaz was very kind to Ruth. He made sure his workers treated Ruth nicely and gave her more grain than she gathered.

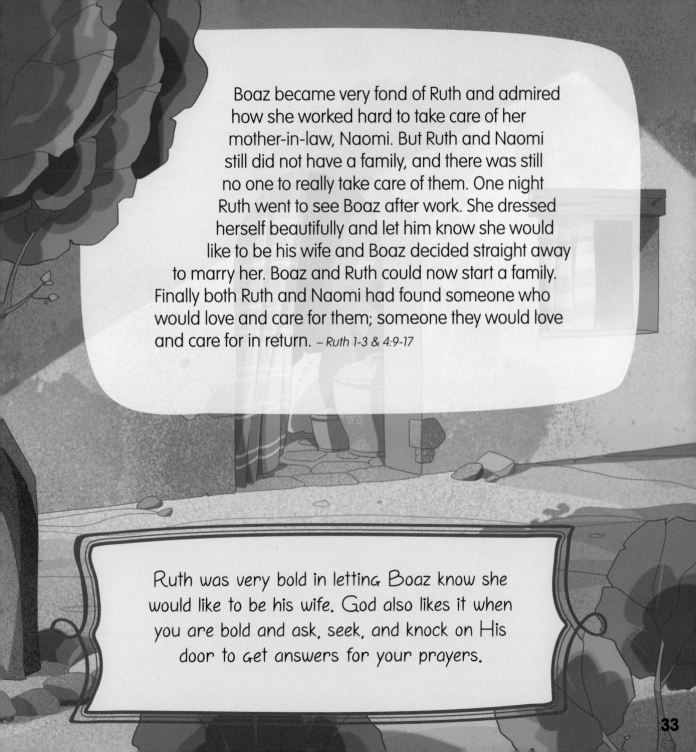

Boaz became very fond of Ruth and admired how she worked hard to take care of her mother-in-law, Naomi. But Ruth and Naomi still did not have a family, and there was still no one to really take care of them. One night Ruth went to see Boaz after work. She dressed herself beautifully and let him know she would like to be his wife and Boaz decided straight away to marry her. Boaz and Ruth could now start a family. Finally both Ruth and Naomi had found someone who would love and care for them; someone they would love and care for in return. *– Ruth 1-3 & 4:9-17*

Ruth was very bold in letting Boaz know she would like to be his wife. God also likes it when you are bold and ask, seek, and knock on His door to Get answers for your prayers.

The LORD is my shepherd;
I have all that I need.

Psalm 23:1 (NLT)

34

## The Shepherd Boy and Warrior King

David was the youngest boy of eight brothers, and he tended his father's sheep. He was a brave shepherd, and He knew God was with him. David was not afraid of fighting lions and bears when they tried to take a sheep from his flock. His brothers didn't think much of David, but God, who knew David perfectly well, saw that David loved Him with all his heart.

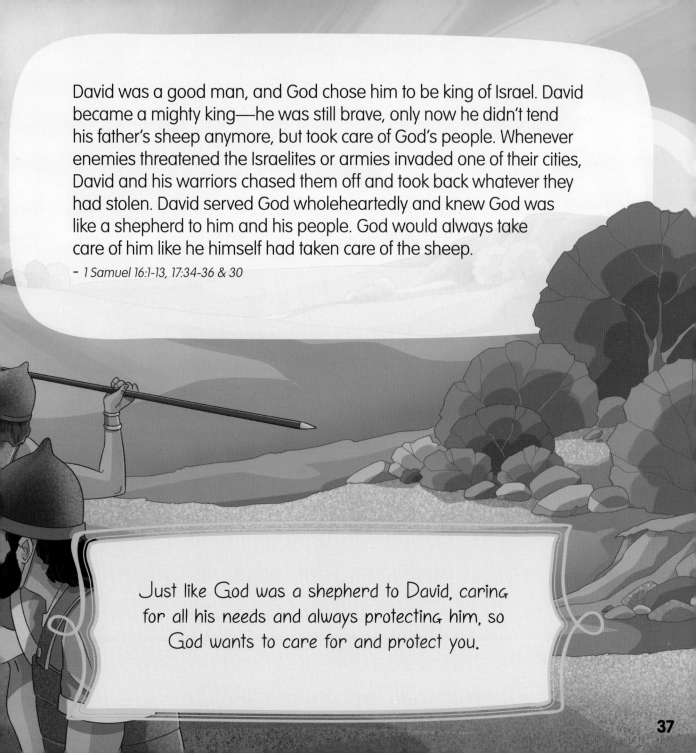

David was a good man, and God chose him to be king of Israel. David became a mighty king—he was still brave, only now he didn't tend his father's sheep anymore, but took care of God's people. Whenever enemies threatened the Israelites or armies invaded one of their cities, David and his warriors chased them off and took back whatever they had stolen. David served God wholeheartedly and knew God was like a shepherd to him and his people. God would always take care of him like he himself had taken care of the sheep.

– *1 Samuel 16:1-13, 17:34-36 & 30*

Just like God was a shepherd to David, caring for all his needs and always protecting him, so God wants to care for and protect you.

Don't worry about anything; instead, pray about everything.

Philippians 4:6 (NLT)

## A Beautiful Queen Saves a Nation

There was once a beautiful Jewish girl named Esther, who was married to the King of Persia. One day Esther heard that a man named Haman had tricked the king into making a law that would have all the Jews in the Persian kingdom killed! Her Jewish family and friends outside the palace were in danger and so was she. Only Esther could get access to the king and beg him to change the law.

Esther knew she could be killed for coming before the king without an invitation, but she had to help her people. Otherwise, who would? She then asked the Jewish people to fast and pray for her for three days. On the third day Esther dressed herself in her finest dress, determined to approach the king, no matter if she lived or died doing it. She feared for her life, but the king had favor on Esther and allowed her to speak with him. So Esther pleaded for the lives of the Jewish people. After realizing what Haman had done, the king made a new law that would save the Jews from their enemies. Esther's bravery had rescued her people! *- Esther 4:1-5:3, 8*

God is a mighty God, and He knows when you feel sad, alone, or even when you're in danger. He wants to help you, and He always hears your prayers.

Love the LORD your God with all your heart and with all your soul and with all your strength.

Deuteronomy 6:5

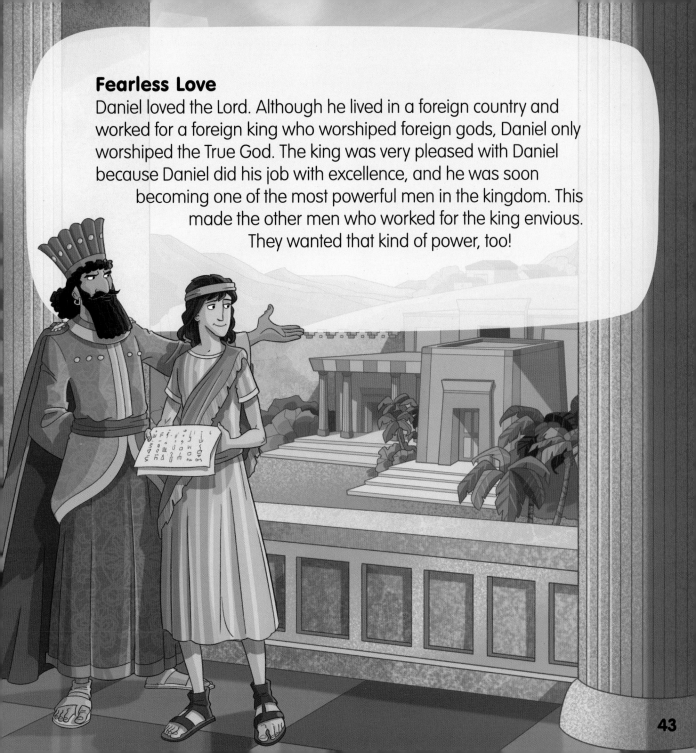

## Fearless Love

Daniel loved the Lord. Although he lived in a foreign country and worked for a foreign king who worshiped foreign gods, Daniel only worshiped the True God. The king was very pleased with Daniel because Daniel did his job with excellence, and he was soon becoming one of the most powerful men in the kingdom. This made the other men who worked for the king envious. They wanted that kind of power, too!

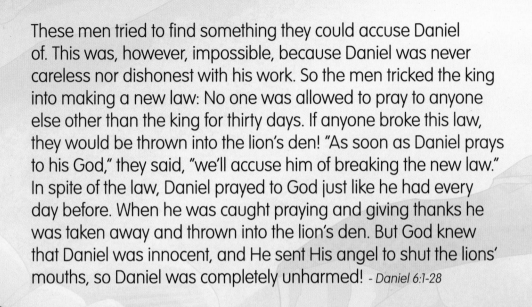

These men tried to find something they could accuse Daniel of. This was, however, impossible, because Daniel was never careless nor dishonest with his work. So the men tricked the king into making a new law: No one was allowed to pray to anyone else other than the king for thirty days. If anyone broke this law, they would be thrown into the lion's den! "As soon as Daniel prays to his God," they said, "we'll accuse him of breaking the new law." In spite of the law, Daniel prayed to God just like he had every day before. When he was caught praying and giving thanks he was taken away and thrown into the lion's den. But God knew that Daniel was innocent, and He sent His angel to shut the lions' mouths, so Daniel was completely unharmed! *- Daniel 6:1-28*

There is nothing too difficult for God to help you with. When you love God with all your heart, soul, and strength it is easier to trust that He will do whatever it takes to protect you.

The LORD is good to all;
He has compassion on all He
has made.

Psalm 145:9

46

## God's Forgiveness

Nineveh was a wicked place. One day God told Jonah to go there to warn the people to turn from their evil ways or God would punish them. But Jonah didn't want to go warn them. He wanted the Ninevites to suffer their punishment, so instead he tried to run away and went by boat in the opposite direction of Nineveh. But God sent a storm and Jonah was thrown into the sea and swallowed by a huge fish. Inside the fish Jonah prayed: "God, I'm sorry. Please help me, and I'll do whatever you ask of me." The fish eventually spit him out and Jonah went to Nineveh.

When the Ninevites heard Jonah's message, they were truly sorry and asked God for forgiveness. Meanwhile Jonah sat outside the city, waiting to see how God would punish the people. But nothing happened! God had understood how sorry the Ninevites were and He had forgiven them. This made Jonah angry—he wanted them to be punished like they deserved. "Why did I come all this way to tell these people of a punishment that would never come?" Jonah grumbled. God then said to him, "Jonah, should I not have compassion on these people now that they have turned from evil? I made these people, and I care for them." And God had mercy on the city of Nineveh and on Jonah, too. - *Jonah 1-4*

God is a good and compassionate God. He loves you very much because He made you. When you do wrong, He is ready to forgive you the minute you ask Him.

Come, let us bow down in worship, let us kneel before the LORD our Maker.

Psalm 95:6

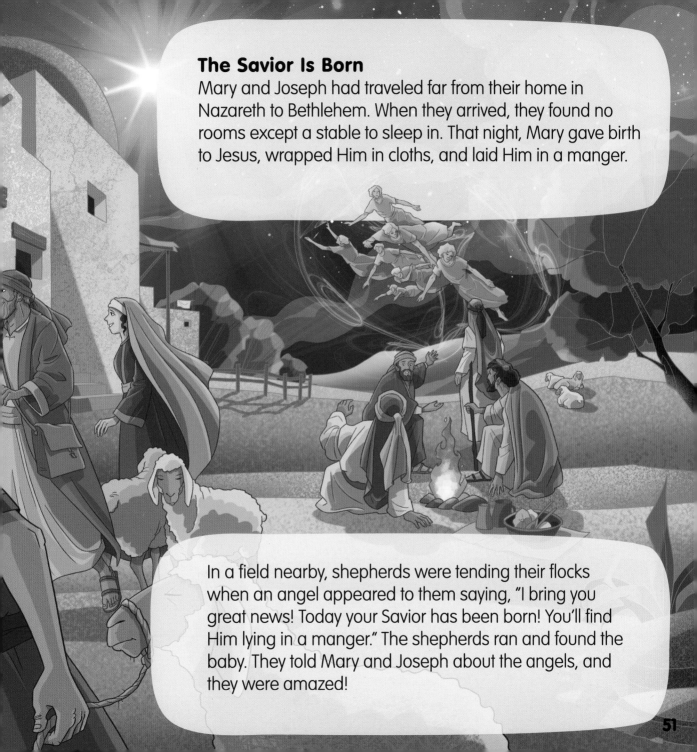

## The Savior Is Born

Mary and Joseph had traveled far from their home in Nazareth to Bethlehem. When they arrived, they found no rooms except a stable to sleep in. That night, Mary gave birth to Jesus, wrapped Him in cloths, and laid Him in a manger.

In a field nearby, shepherds were tending their flocks when an angel appeared to them saying, "I bring you great news! Today your Savior has been born! You'll find Him lying in a manger." The shepherds ran and found the baby. They told Mary and Joseph about the angels, and they were amazed!

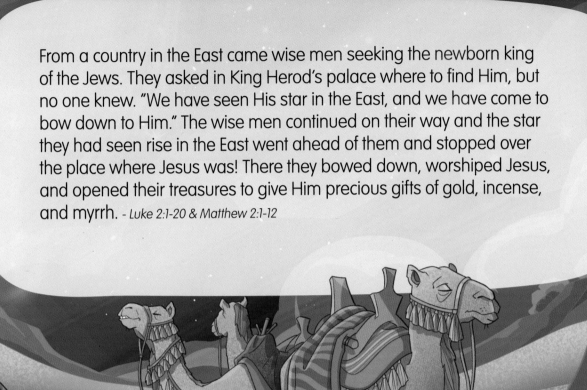

From a country in the East came wise men seeking the newborn king of the Jews. They asked in King Herod's palace where to find Him, but no one knew. "We have seen His star in the East, and we have come to bow down to Him." The wise men continued on their way and the star they had seen rise in the East went ahead of them and stopped over the place where Jesus was! There they bowed down, worshiped Jesus, and opened their treasures to give Him precious gifts of gold, incense, and myrrh. *- Luke 2:1-20 & Matthew 2:1-12*

The shepherds and the wise men knew that Jesus was their Lord and Savior and they bowed down to Him in worship. You can give praise and say thanks to Jesus for being your Savior, too.

Give thanks to the LORD,
for He is good;
His love endures forever.

Psalm 107:1

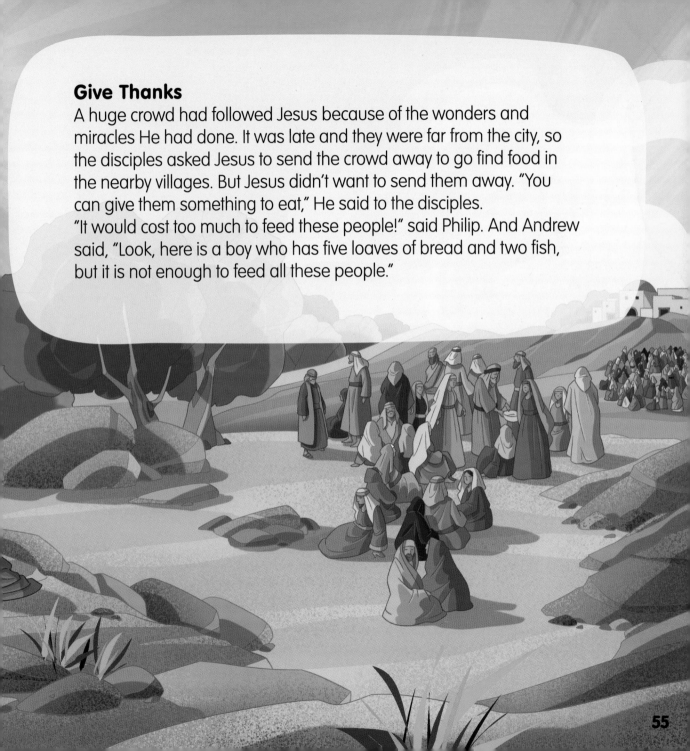

## Give Thanks

A huge crowd had followed Jesus because of the wonders and miracles He had done. It was late and they were far from the city, so the disciples asked Jesus to send the crowd away to go find food in the nearby villages. But Jesus didn't want to send them away. "You can give them something to eat," He said to the disciples.

"It would cost too much to feed these people!" said Philip. And Andrew said, "Look, here is a boy who has five loaves of bread and two fish, but it is not enough to feed all these people."

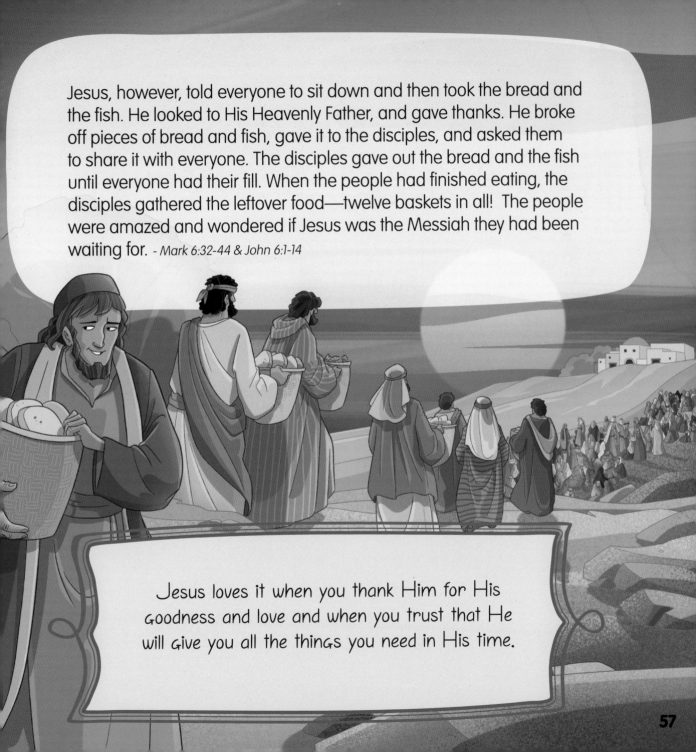

Jesus, however, told everyone to sit down and then took the bread and the fish. He looked to His Heavenly Father, and gave thanks. He broke off pieces of bread and fish, gave it to the disciples, and asked them to share it with everyone. The disciples gave out the bread and the fish until everyone had their fill. When the people had finished eating, the disciples gathered the leftover food—twelve baskets in all! The people were amazed and wondered if Jesus was the Messiah they had been waiting for. *- Mark 6:32-44 & John 6:1-14*

Jesus loves it when you thank Him for His goodness and love and when you trust that He will give you all the things you need in His time.

57

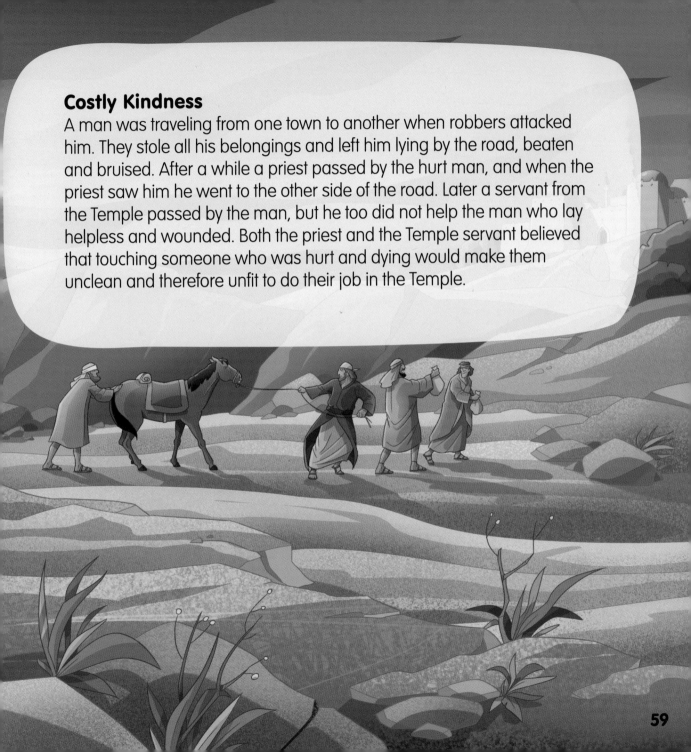

## Costly Kindness

A man was traveling from one town to another when robbers attacked him. They stole all his belongings and left him lying by the road, beaten and bruised. After a while a priest passed by the hurt man, and when the priest saw him he went to the other side of the road. Later a servant from the Temple passed by the man, but he too did not help the man who lay helpless and wounded. Both the priest and the Temple servant believed that touching someone who was hurt and dying would make them unclean and therefore unfit to do their job in the Temple.

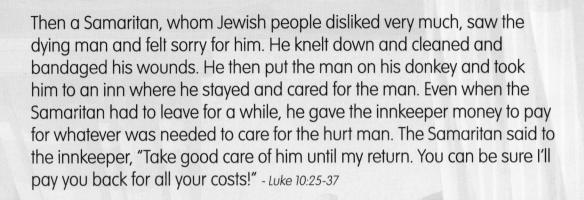

Then a Samaritan, whom Jewish people disliked very much, saw the dying man and felt sorry for him. He knelt down and cleaned and bandaged his wounds. He then put the man on his donkey and took him to an inn where he stayed and cared for the man. Even when the Samaritan had to leave for a while, he gave the innkeeper money to pay for whatever was needed to care for the hurt man. The Samaritan said to the innkeeper, "Take good care of him until my return. You can be sure I'll pay you back for all your costs!" - *Luke 10:25-37*

Sometimes it is difficult or costly to care for others. Sometimes it takes time away from doing something else. But being kind to others, no matter who they are, is acting like God and doing so makes you become more like Him.

Be kind and compassionate to one another, forgiving each other, just as in Christ God forgave you.

Ephesians 4:32

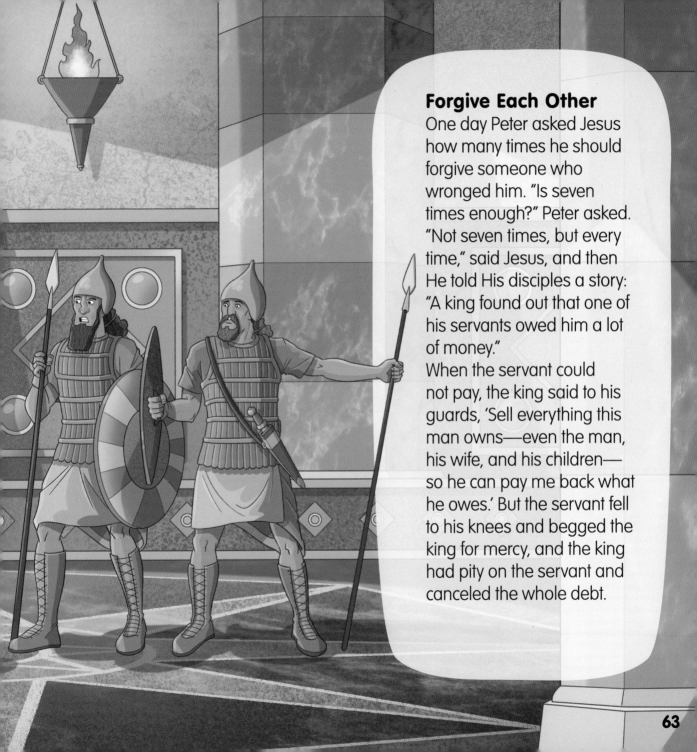

## Forgive Each Other

One day Peter asked Jesus how many times he should forgive someone who wronged him. "Is seven times enough?" Peter asked. "Not seven times, but every time," said Jesus, and then He told His disciples a story: "A king found out that one of his servants owed him a lot of money."

When the servant could not pay, the king said to his guards, 'Sell everything this man owns—even the man, his wife, and his children—so he can pay me back what he owes.' But the servant fell to his knees and begged the king for mercy, and the king had pity on the servant and canceled the whole debt.

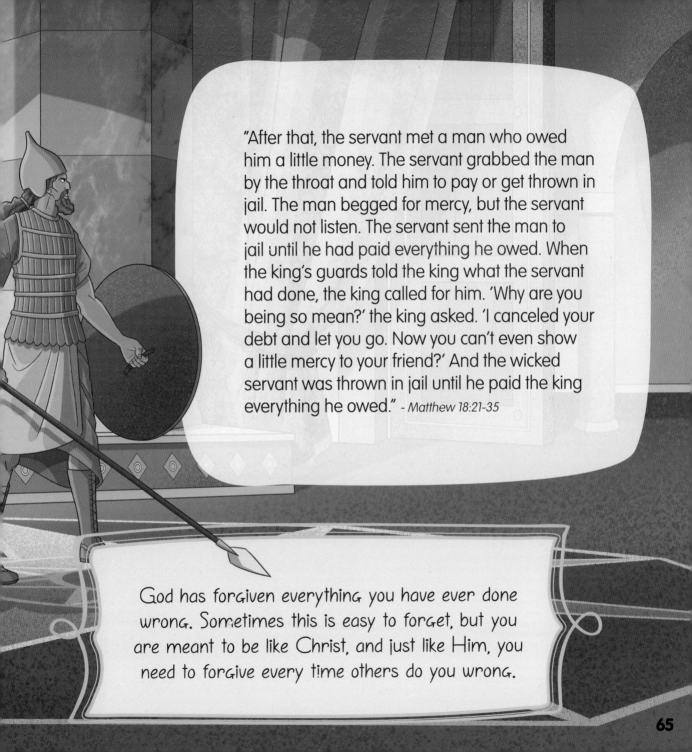

"After that, the servant met a man who owed him a little money. The servant grabbed the man by the throat and told him to pay or get thrown in jail. The man begged for mercy, but the servant would not listen. The servant sent the man to jail until he had paid everything he owed. When the king's guards told the king what the servant had done, the king called for him. 'Why are you being so mean?' the king asked. 'I canceled your debt and let you go. Now you can't even show a little mercy to your friend?' And the wicked servant was thrown in jail until he paid the king everything he owed." - *Matthew 18:21-35*

God has forgiven everything you have ever done wrong. Sometimes this is easy to forget, but you are meant to be like Christ, and just like Him, you need to forgive every time others do you wrong.

"Let the little children come to me, and do not hinder them, for the Kingdom of God belongs to such as these".

Luke 18:16

## Come to Me

One day when Jesus was teaching, some people brought their babies and young children to Him. They wanted Jesus to lay His hands on their children and bless them. The disciples started to shoo the people away. But Jesus said to the disciples, "Let the children come to me!"

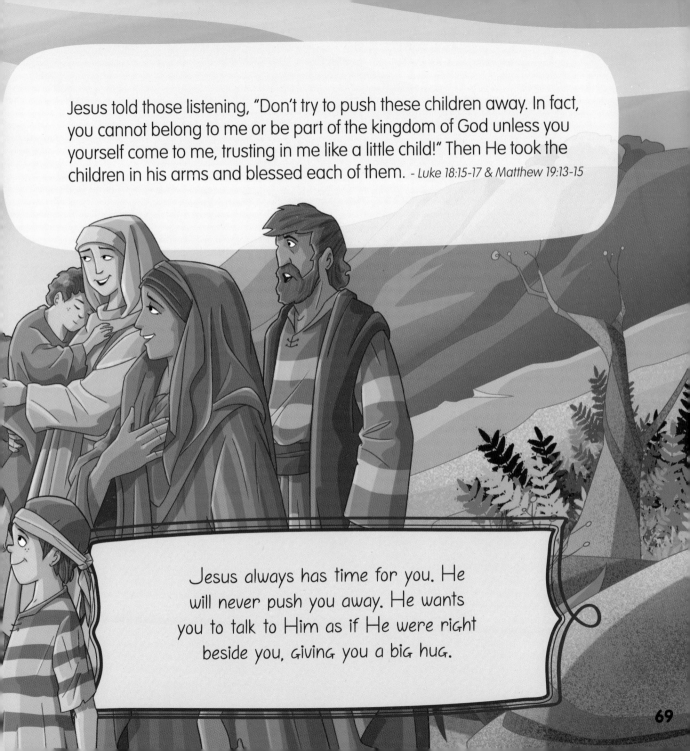

Jesus told those listening, "Don't try to push these children away. In fact, you cannot belong to me or be part of the kingdom of God unless you yourself come to me, trusting in me like a little child!" Then He took the children in his arms and blessed each of them. *- Luke 18:15-17 & Matthew 19:13-15*

Jesus always has time for you. He will never push you away. He wants you to talk to Him as if He were right beside you, giving you a big hug.

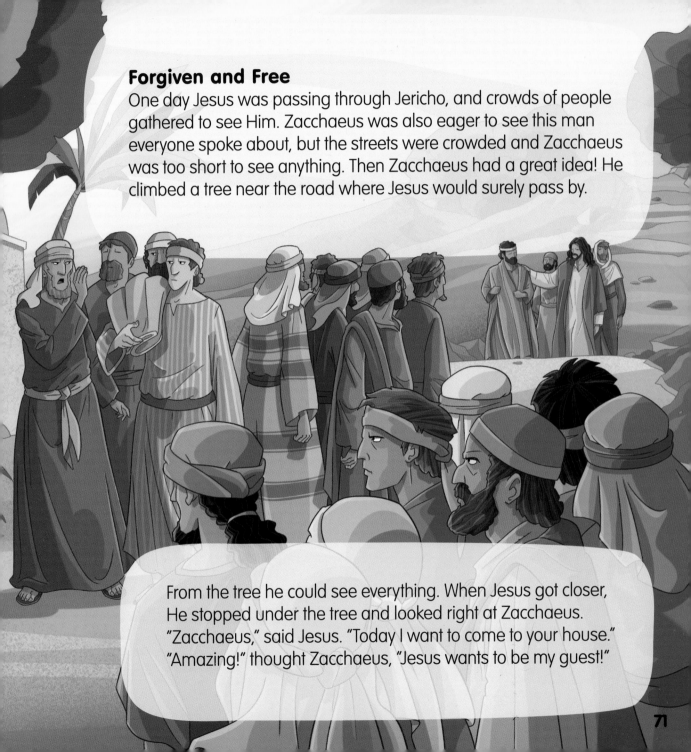

## Forgiven and Free

One day Jesus was passing through Jericho, and crowds of people gathered to see Him. Zacchaeus was also eager to see this man everyone spoke about, but the streets were crowded and Zacchaeus was too short to see anything. Then Zacchaeus had a great idea! He climbed a tree near the road where Jesus would surely pass by.

From the tree he could see everything. When Jesus got closer, He stopped under the tree and looked right at Zacchaeus. "Zacchaeus," said Jesus. "Today I want to come to your house." "Amazing!" thought Zacchaeus, "Jesus wants to be my guest!"

But the people of Jericho were upset. Nobody liked Zacchaeus because he was a money collector for the Romans. The Romans were enemies of the Jews; they were foreigners ruling Israel and forcing them to pay taxes to their emperor in Rome. Was Jesus really going to visit Zacchaeus?

But Zacchaeus was beaming with happiness as he said, "I'll give half my belongings to the poor, and if I ever cheated anyone, I'll pay him back four times." Jesus smiled and said to the other guests, "Today, this man has been forgiven. It is people like Zacchaeus whom I came to seek and save." - *Luke 19:1-10*

When you ask God to forgive you, God will remember your sins no more. Then you will be free from the sin in your heart and you can do the good things God wants you to do.

For God so loved the world that He gave His one and only Son, that whoever believes in Him shall not perish but have eternal life.

John 3:16

## Jesus Made a Way

Israel's religious leaders hated Jesus, and they schemed to kill Him. They were jealous because many people loved Him and angry that He claimed to be God's Son. According to Jewish law, claiming to be the Son of God was a sin and should be punished by death. Even when they accused Jesus of things He had not done, He didn't try to save Himself from suffering or death. When they put Him on the cross, insulted Him, and laughed at Him, He asked God to forgive them. As Jesus died, the veil in the Temple, which had separated the people from God, ripped in two.

Jesus had made a way for people to come to God. Now everyone who believes that Jesus is the Son of God can come to God freely—just like a child would run to their father or mother. Jesus, who did nothing wrong and could not be blamed for anything, had taken all our blame and guilt upon Himself. He received the punishment for our sins in our stead. God loved the world so much that He was willing to give up His precious and perfect Son to be punished for our sin. Now, we can have eternal life and be with God forever because of what Jesus did for us on the cross. *- Matthew 27:11-56, Luke 23 & Isaiah 53*

God loves you so much that He gave His Son for you. There is nothing He wants more than for you to open your heart to His love and receive Him as your Savior.

"I am the resurrection and the life. Anyone who believes in me will live, even after dying."

John 11:25 (NLT)

### Jesus Is Alive!

On the third day after Jesus had been crucified, Mary Magdalene went to Jesus' tomb to grieve. When she arrived she saw that the stone had been rolled away and the grave was empty! Mary was very troubled by this. Where had they taken her Lord? As she wept she looked into the tomb, and right there, where Jesus' body had been, two angels were sitting. "Why are you crying?" they asked and Mary said, "Someone has taken my Jesus away and I don't know where they have put him."

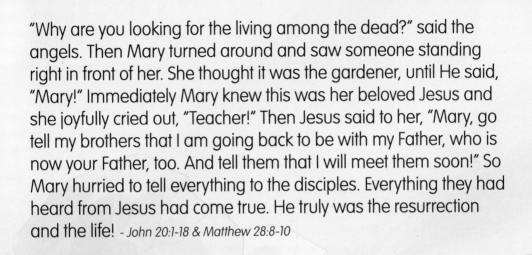

"Why are you looking for the living among the dead?" said the angels. Then Mary turned around and saw someone standing right in front of her. She thought it was the gardener, until He said, "Mary!" Immediately Mary knew this was her beloved Jesus and she joyfully cried out, "Teacher!" Then Jesus said to her, "Mary, go tell my brothers that I am going back to be with my Father, who is now your Father, too. And tell them that I will meet them soon!" So Mary hurried to tell everything to the disciples. Everything they had heard from Jesus had come true. He truly was the resurrection and the life! - *John 20:1-18 & Matthew 28:8-10*

When you believe in Jesus, He has promised you eternal life. He won over death, so you will never have to fear dying.

## God Takes Care of His Followers

The first believers in Christ grew in number and soon they were a community of people living life together. They loved Jesus and took care of each other. No one kept anything for themselves, but everyone shared what they had with those in need. Some Christians who owned land and houses sold them and gave the money to the apostles. The apostles then gave the money to those who needed it. God's grace worked in their hearts, and in time there was no needy person among them.

A wealthy man named Joseph sold his land and gave the money to the apostles to help others. Joseph was also known as Barnabas, which means Son of Encouragement. Later Barnabas became a great teacher and prophet, and he traveled with other Christians to preach the good news all over the region. They told people about the Kingdom of God and what Jesus had done for them on the cross. Because of Barnabas and his fellow Christians, many people believed and came to faith in Jesus. - *Acts 4:32-37, 11:22-26 & 13:1-3*

When you trust God and live your life
to please Him, He will give you all the
things you really need.

If we believe that Jesus is truly Christ, we are God's children.

1 John 5:1 (CEV)

## Changed by the Truth

As the number of believers grew, so did their problems. Many people despised Christians. One man worked especially hard to put Christians in prison or even to death. His name was Saul. He was a Jew and knew God, but He didn't believe Jesus Christ was His Son, and Saul persecuted those who did. Christians fled far from their homes in order to be safe.

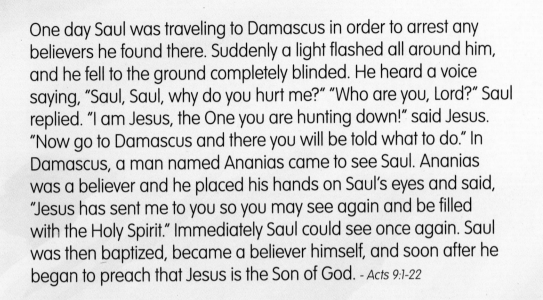

One day Saul was traveling to Damascus in order to arrest any believers he found there. Suddenly a light flashed all around him, and he fell to the ground completely blinded. He heard a voice saying, "Saul, Saul, why do you hurt me?" "Who are you, Lord?" Saul replied. "I am Jesus, the One you are hunting down!" said Jesus. "Now go to Damascus and there you will be told what to do." In Damascus, a man named Ananias came to see Saul. Ananias was a believer and he placed his hands on Saul's eyes and said, "Jesus has sent me to you so you may see again and be filled with the Holy Spirit." Immediately Saul could see once again. Saul was then baptized, became a believer himself, and soon after he began to preach that Jesus is the Son of God. - *Acts 9:1-22*

If you believe that Jesus is the Son of God who came to die for your sins, you, too, are a child of God.

Rejoice in the Lord always.
I will say it again: Rejoice!

Philippians 4:4

## Sing Praise to God

Saul, who was later called Paul, traveled around Israel and the surrounding countries telling people about Jesus. On one such trip he brought a fellow believer called Silas and they traveled to a town called Philippi. There they got into big trouble for sharing their faith and performing miracles. Paul and Silas were beaten up and thrown into the deepest, darkest part of the prison, where their feet were put in stocks. In spite of this, Paul and Silas prayed and sang songs to God, and the other prisoners listened to them.

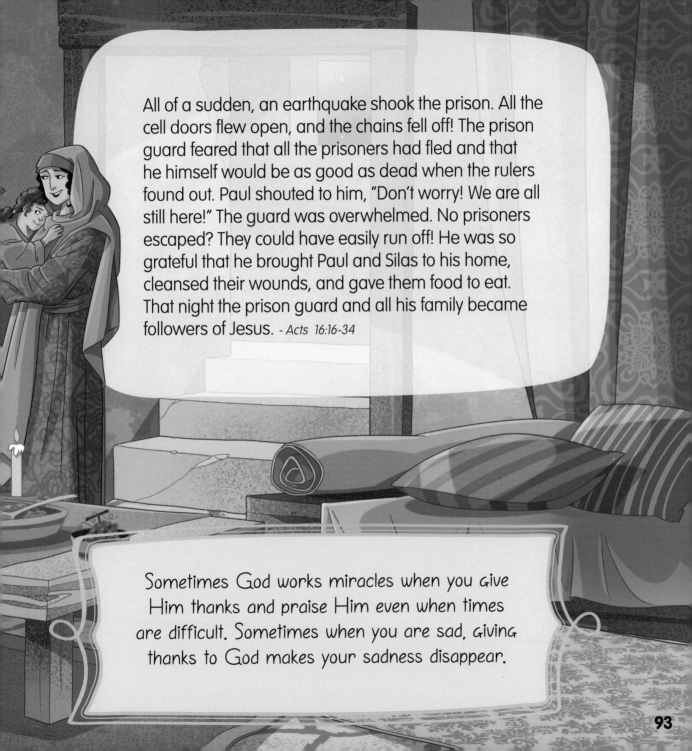

All of a sudden, an earthquake shook the prison. All the cell doors flew open, and the chains fell off! The prison guard feared that all the prisoners had fled and that he himself would be as good as dead when the rulers found out. Paul shouted to him, "Don't worry! We are all still here!" The guard was overwhelmed. No prisoners escaped? They could have easily run off! He was so grateful that he brought Paul and Silas to his home, cleansed their wounds, and gave them food to eat. That night the prison guard and all his family became followers of Jesus. - *Acts 16:16-34*

Sometimes God works miracles when you give Him thanks and praise Him even when times are difficult. Sometimes when you are sad, giving thanks to God makes your sadness disappear.